# River of Light

# River of Light

Prose & Poetry
by
**Jasmine Kang**

**So'ham Books**

**So'ham Books**
48 Vikas Vihar
Ambala City - 134 003, Haryana, India.
*Email:* sohambooks@gmail.com
*Website:* http://www.geocities.com/sohambooks
*Blog:* http://sohambooks.blogspot.com

First Edition 2009
ISBN-13: 978-81-904818-3-0
ISBN-10: 81-904818-3-5



Cover art and author's portrait by Wendy Williams



So'ham, in Sanskrit, means I am God. So'ham Books, the publishing house, attempts to cater to the readers' need for quality books. Although poetry is our area of focus, we are open to all forms of creative writing.

## Praise for River of Light

"Jasmine Kang writes with a delicate, youthful and joyous observation of life. It is bound to bring a new awareness to our own views of how life goes on around us. Read her poems and lines of thought and pick up a lighter shade of thinking."

**-Stephen Knapp, Author of 15 books on India's culture, www.stephen-knapp.com**

"Excellent, Superb, Fantastic! Jasmine's work is inspirational, straight-from-the-heart, and yet simple. It makes you realize that indeed life is beautiful."

**-Sunny Moza, Filmmaker/Actor, www.sunnymoza.com**

"River of Light by Jasmine Kang is an ode to a painted beauty called "life". Even in the face of despair the poet teaches us to not lose sight that despair and sorrow are only a small part of the richness we call life. Jasmine refuses to see life apart from the activity of art, just as art and the artist are inseparable. Whatever the artist creates she's recreating her relationship with her surroundings within the realm of oneness. While articulating such complex ideas the poet reminds herself and the artist in her readers that whatever we are, whatever we create it is still within the larger realm of Being. Her sense of humility cannot be more direct, beautiful and profound when she says, 'Remember, you are just a drop of the Sea'. By keeping this connection in mind, the despair and sorrow we may dwell on, is not larger than the rest of humanity of which we are only a small part. The rest is life. Jasmine Kang has made a delicious feast out of life for the readers' eyes."

**-Moazzam Sheikh, Author of The Idol Lover & Editor of A Letter from India, http://moazzamsheikh.blogspot.com**

"Jasmine Kang is a creative, talented, and focused poet. Her poems, stories, artwork, and photography are very uplifting. She focuses on waking up our feelings and reminds everyone of the beauty that surrounds us. Through poetry and prose, Jasmine Kang teaches humanity what we should appreciate in life's purpose."

**-Ana Monnar, Author of poetry and children's books and Editor of Express Yourself 101, www.monnar.net**

"River of Light is truly an ocean of wisdom through the eyes of an exceptional writer. Jasmine's words provide the reader with a vivid imagination to dream life into reality. Her self-evident writing style and beautifully crafted artwork will fill the reader with a vision of her simplistic beauty. This book of wisdom and splendid art will remain a priceless gem that Jasmine has bestowed upon the world to read and believe. This River of Light sings forth a song of praise and strength throughout our beautiful days."

**-Mary Battle, Author of A Lifetime of Treasures & Perfumed Legacy, www.lifetimeoftreasures.com**

"Jasmine Kang's book, River of Light, reflects nature, the beauty of life, love, and devotion. The description of nature in her poems is very beautiful and vivid. It inspires the reader to think of the Creator. Jasmine has a profound message in her poems. She tells us that we do not have to search for fulfillment outside in the world--we have it in our hearts. We have to open to our inner Self to experience it. That moment will be the best in our lives. I highly recommend this book."

**-Usha Srivastava, Author of Shraddhanjali: An Offering of Reverence, http://offeringofreverence.googlepages.com**

"River of Light allows readers to pursue their inner self and how this inner self is connected to the reality around them. It is a book that shows beauty and sensitivity. As the author's first book, everything she has learned by searching her inner self and the world around her, writing her findings poetically, submitting poems to publishers and seeing them in print has come to full realization. As editor of theEclectics series of Creative With Words Publications, I encourage lovers of poetry to read River of Light and enjoy the depth with which the author has approached the many poetic themes in her writing."

**-Brigitta Geltrich, Editor, Creative With Words, http://members.tripod.com/~CreativeWithWords**

"Jasmine Kang takes us on a journey with her poetry of life. Too often we are so caught up in the act of existing that we forget what it means to live. Through her words we take the time to move away from "if only" to realize what "is". Her poetry sings the song that life is around us and we need to take the time to recognize what it means to really live."

**-Tom Worthen, Editor, Creative Communication, www.poeticpower.com**

## Dedication

Once I came across a quote by Kelly Jeppesen, "What you are is God's gift to you. What you make of yourself is your gift to God." I realized how true this was. This is my gift.

For Family, Friends & Teachers,
For Love, Life, Peace, Happiness & Truth,
And the One Supreme that made me so...
This is my Flower to You.

# Contents

## Acknowledgements

I would like to express my sincere thanks and appreciation to:

God for carrying me through this project which would not have been possible without the blessings and mercy of the Supreme.

My dear family for all the love and care you have given me throughout the years.

Poonam & Samartha Vashishtha, my editors and collaborators at So'ham Books.

Kristene Fortier for looking over my proposal. Shauna Moriarty, Surya & Isa Vitalis, Ana Monnar, Mary Battle, Brigatta Geltrich, Stephen Knapp, Moazzam Sheikh, Tom Worthen and Usha Srivastava for reviewing my work. Wendy Williams and Bethany McVay for your images. Cesar Lazo, Chad Liffmann and Parag Sankhe for helping spread the word through your film work and creativity. Gabriel Lazo, Alex Orellana, Luminesense and Heidi Seigell for your music.

Friends, especially Cindy, Aiko, Sunny and Prema. Thank you for your support, understanding and for simply being there. Your time, energy, belief, encouragement and feedback lovingly nurtured this project.

And to all others, here and there, who have made this book possible, thank you.

## Foreword

A glimpse into life that is truly alive

Would you like partake in the miracle of life? Do you believe words can wash the dust from your eye so that you may see anew? You are invited to invoke beauty and resonate with the suchness of each moment. You may recall your enraptured senses of childhood still reverberating in the timeless fields of curving space. Truly, heaven on earth exists for those that have eyes to see and ears to hear. All we need is a quiet heart and a fresh look. The invitation reverberates in these poems… "come and taste heaven again with me."

Aware and awake to the beauty of life, Jasmine lovingly offers her heartfelt gift in these pages. How refreshing to look once more through the eyes of innocent wonder, gratitude, and poetic sensitivity! Living pictures alive with genuine experience sanctify the moment, and reveal the poet's awareness of her consciousness as it plays and touches the mind's holographic nature. A door opens to the plane of subtle observation, where we can watch scenes and images dance on the screen of consciousness, and become aware of the screen itself, the backdrop to the play.

Curiosity, wonder, and discovery live in these pages. When sensuality abides in purity, there is divine ecstasy, a heart so full that beautiful words and images flow spontaneously from the mountain. The songs of love must be shared, the connection of all life celebrated, and so a poet seeks again and again to find words to paint an image of our vast connection with the universe and all beings.

The first pressing of the olives' fragrant oil, with all the essences so fresh upon our senses, is a sacred moment repeated anew with every poem. Time is not a relentless wheel but a blissful rhythm of the seasons. In autumn, nature promises the flowery overtones of spring to be hidden in the oil's delicate scent. Wherever we walk, we press the wine under our feet. You will miss the moment, or you will taste it.

These poems invite you to taste, yes, taste your life, your connection again.

Jasmine's images celebrate a life of vibrant colors not just seen but lived with a heart washed in the waters of gratitude. Her poems remind us that life is a sacred gift. Every moment beckons.

Enter here through the door marked "Know thyself"...

**Surya Vitalis**

**Musician and Songwriter**
**www.clearlightmusic.com**

## Introduction

It is all here, inside of you.
Start from here
And you will find everything else
You are looking for.

There is a dream in each one of us, to be something, to share something with the world. Each one of us has a gift to offer to the world. River of Light is a realization and quest of discovery of life, oneself, one's purpose and what it means to be alive, capturing the depth, vastness and beauty of life through prose and poetry. It is a spiritual journey from dreams to self-fulfillment focusing on our place in the world, our connection to the world, reminding ourselves of the dreamer in us, the great beauty of life and the hope that we are capable of achieving our dreams.

Every story has to start somewhere. This story starts at the heart of being, the very life and beauty in us. As children, we dream. As we grow up and pass through that stage, the dream is still there, but we become so caught up with different tasks that believing itself becomes hard and we forget what it means to live. This is a story of a dreamer, the dreamer in us, who wakes up and finds that dreams can become reality.

I woke up with a dream in my heart. I had felt the light and warmth of the sun on my eyes. I opened my eyes, saw the golden light of the sun peaking in through the window and thought, "Why are we always looking for something else when that happiness is already there?" All of our lives, we seem to be searching for something...to find it was there all along, our dream. We look for happiness, but we find that the happiness we think to be really isn't. It's then that part of life we had put behind comes back to us and we remember our dream again.

## Beauty of Nature

I saw a flower
And it touched my heart
I etched its picture onto my mind
That I could not forget

There is a moment that pulls
A moment that we want
To be forever
Whatever it is
That one moment gives
What another cannot
See it in the beauty of nature
The stars are coming out
And their twinkles are like
The flames of a fire

## Silently

Silently,
One by one,
In the infinite
Meadows of heaven
Blossomed the lovely
Stars, the forget-me-nots
Of angels

## Together

I look outside the window,
see the sun setting,
and the color of the sun's light fading,
always together.
Our connections cannot be abandoned.
How we come,
share the golden beam
that links us all together is art.
A painter gazes at the amber mountains
in the horizon overlooking the clear sky.
A painter views the changing indigo colors,
hues of violet that are portrayed
by the coming of a sunset:
swirls of fiery scarlet, golden and orange
lit up with a touch of amethyst.
Nature makes one wonder,
wonder does the painter
as the winds remain constant,
marveling with inspiration,
the moment is caught and painted
onto a canvas portrayed
into a long lived memory
for generations to come.
And sweet memories these will remain
as the colors melt all differences
into complete oneness.
There are no walls of separation.

## Art that touches bliss

Art that touches bliss
An expression of this freedom
Impressions of what is seen, felt
Inspiring me, a muse, a touch
A quest, sharing moments
Reflections, understanding
All the possibilities of life
In you, before you

## An Artist and His Creation

See the painting an artist paints
with its colors and their contrasts
that the radiance of the sun gives off
Watch the artist as he plays with color

As the artist paints,
he creates his own reality
He needs only inspiration
All boundaries between dream
and reality are dissolved

Every color has existence
as we give it existence
making our dream real

## Sweet as the nectar

Sweet as the nectar, honey of a bee,
Aromatic as jasmines,
And the spikes of lilac-purple flowers,
Lavender,
And crimson roses, marigolds,
And sandal... O, sweetness divine!

When the moon shines bright
And a cool breeze gently blows,
There I find magic in the air
And music everywhere
As we meet crafting dreams
Out of our one dream of life.

Does the beauty of the rose eventually die out?
I bear these memories of the past seasons
In a stream of consciousness: I see
Colors of day breaking,
Autumn colors like fallen leaves
Along the banks of the river,
Fields of saffron flowers blooming,
And in the winter, hills of pine and alpine
Meadows amidst dramatic mountain gorges,
And then, colors echoing the yellow
Mustard blossoms in bloom
In the fertile plains in spring,
A carpet of anemones, roses,
Wild irises, lavenders and alpine flora,
Blue poppies, and lovely white blossoms
From the cherry trees.
With summer there are savannah grasslands,
Lush pastures and hilly ridges
With sal-laden forests.

I see every autumn oil lamps
Floating on riverbanks at eve,
And the stained-glass windows of perception
From which I view the beauty
Of day and night.

Where does all of beauty lie?
I looked at the mirror and saw myself,
But the self is deeper than this.
When you are gone,
No longer will this face be, but you will be.
And so the flowers wither with time,
You remember the fragrance they leave.
The essence doesn't die.

From dawn to dusk and again day breaks,
There comes evening and a night to slumber.
Like a summer's day, long and unending
This song in its eternity of forever

My muses have been stirred
By a painted beauty called "life".
With the sun and the moon,
With the earth and all its richness,
With all delights of the seasons,
I am stirred again by this
Sweet silence.
What if time came to a standstill?
You still have the present moment!

With kajjala round her eyes,
Hair as golden hued as the sun
And lips of crimson rose
Like the red in coral,
Cheeks laden with a blush of scarlet

And skin soft white as a pearl,
She holds roses damasked
As an offering before the Divine.

I sense something far more
In depth than can be said.
It is a painted beauty of life,
Sweet as the nectar
Of the flowers
She offered.

**A Flower for You**

It is a gift,
Within me, around me,
The breath of life
It sings within me,
All around me
I hear it
In the songs of the birds,
I smell it
In the sweetness of fragrance
Emitted by flowers
In the air,
I see it
In the day and night sky,
In oneness
And all differences

It is the gift of every
Form, possibility
The gift of all that is Existence
Every face holds the gift of you, Life
The branches of the trees

Every face is a wonder in itself
With Love inside
When you see and realize
There is beauty
Life opens up
Like a flower for you

**The Picture I Painted of You**

The scent of a flower,
The shadows on the wall,
The picture I painted of you...

A wind enveloped around me
As I watched the slow movement
Of the ocean waves
Along the shores of the beach.
I saw seashells, pebbles, seaweed, kelp,
Charcoal and a kite on wet sand.

I remember those summer days
When people went to the beach for a stroll,
And all the kite flying...
I would collect seashells
And charcoal to sketch a picture of you.

The artist paints a picture of you.
Sing, sing, sweet melody.

The wind stole away the warmth
I had and the waters washed away
What was scattered here and there
As I painted a picture of you.
But you are the Life of the sun,
The Light of the lighthouse

In the sky. You need no other light.

The wind diffused the scent,
Dried what was once a flower
To bits destined to become
A part of the vastness of the sea.
But you are that flower of love undying,
Never fading,
That stream ever flowing
In a state of bliss divine and harmony
Always for the eternity of forever.

It was the picture I painted of you.

Against the rising sun, atop the edge of the hill,
She sits with her gaze upon
The canvas set before her
The world that sits below her is of the moors.
Overhead is a canopy
Of early morning light.

Pull the curtains and see yourself
Looking through a window.
Look through the looking glass
And what do you see
On the other side?
The picture I painted of you.

I hold my hand out
With a flower for you.
Love is my soul,
My dharma, my life.
It is the way of life,
The way to coming together.

Glistening on granite,

Our love is etched.
Hear the symphony of songbirds.
It is the song of our love.

Life and its richness
Caressing me...
Sing, sing, sweet melody.

Feel the wind
The rain
It all fills my mind with such wonder.

I stepped into a painting,
Followed you
Inside
Only to lose sight of you,
But to find that you were
Always there, never gone.

I walked out of the painting
Into the shadows.
I found myself wandering
In the footsteps of my past,
My childhood, into a free world
Filled with wonder and awe.
See the innocence of a child.

Make the sun shine for me,
Like the life of it you are.

The universe is like so many worlds
Put together into one photograph.
Your Consciousness is a universe in itself.

Life is a never ending album,

A motion picture from day one.
But who is to say that was the start?
What beginning do you speak of?
I know none.

It is all eternal, never ending.
Incarnations past, lives to come and go...
Capture the images.
You are what you are.
And that was it, the picture I painted
Of you, already there
Painted by the Light of you.

## A Living Drama

Ah, life, what a life, such is this dream,
like the flower that blooms in summer,
and then withers away in winter!
Here I be today, and tomorrow be I gone,
like the wind that sweeps away with it
fallen leaves of autumn, and the present moment
stands still, infinite, eternal, creating a tapestry
to be remembered and to be forgotten.
Like art it is, this living drama with its painted hues of a brush,
radiating rays from the touch of divine light,
bringing meaning to the living tapestry of our lives.
What is to be known? And what is to be forgotten?
Yonder she looks to the sky and the moonlight
that reflects itself upon the blue of the night.
What beauty lies hither and there in complete oneness,
like the beams of the sun that connect with each other,
and the constellations in the heavens.
Ah, life, what a life! And the disguises that come with it!

And the tapestry lives on with its reminiscences.
Rich is this art that we call "life".

*Note: Previously published in "A Celebration of Young Poets" (Spring 2002 edition) by Creative Communication.*

**Life is like music**

Every song is a chapter in our lives. Make it beautiful as any other.

With every song sung, every tear shed, the changing seasons, sunshine and rain, with every passing cloud, life keeps changing and with that time.

Every emotion, feeling, heartbeat after heartbeat, waking, sleeping, day after day, life.

So much to experience, so much to feel.

We smile, we laugh, we cry. All these emotions, like a great dance pulling us in and out. Life. And then it makes us stop and wonder. Life. We are like the stars that dance in the sky, each shining its own story.

Sometimes things aren't the same anymore. Just as dawn's early light comes, evening's moonlight comes, and in life's path comes joy and sorrow.

But did you ever think, what if in life there was only bliss, then how would we ever understand this?! And did you ever think if there was no joy, then what would happen?!

Life is like that beautiful flower you see, but even that flower is changing. That is the great beauty of it. Here we are in a life just as beautiful. Breathe. See. Touch. Hear. Smell. Taste. Feel it in every way. Every moment is infinite in itself with so many possibilities. Life is always there waiting for you. Let it embrace you. There is so much here! Believe.

*Note: Previously published in "What is the Meaning of Life?" (June 2009) by Scott Hoops.*

## You see with your eyes

You see with your eyes
You see the world
Sometimes, it's not so clear
But even then, something's there
It's faith, hope, inner strength
And belief that keeps you going

Sometimes, the picture isn't so clear,
But it's there, all complete
And life seems so complete
Like all pieces of the puzzle
Have been put together
And now I just wonder
You see with your eyes
You see the world
It's all complete now

## Something More

We can love or we can hate.
We can free our minds or fall down.
We can have differences

Or we can be One.

Rise, arise, open your eyes.
There is something more.
Breath after breath, second after second,
Open up your eyes.
And you will see something more.
We're all spirits walking with the Light.

Take a single blade of grass
And you will see beauty
As you behold yourself in the moment
With the greatness of nature and all of life.

Look outside at the trees, at the sky.
Remember, you are just a drop of the Sea,
Just a single drop of the Sea.

### Finding myself

Finding myself coming home
a warm sunrise like a light bathing
in a pool of blue with a soft glow
colors changing, yellow with the sunlight
fields green, groves dancing before my eyes
kites in the sky, monsoon rains, my eyes open

ethereal, wispy morning mist
trees stepping in and out
of warm pools of the bright sun
brown earth falling away

the river dances, listen to the sound
of soft wind through the trees

fields immense
pure bliss
dawning lavender-pink sky
slopes of green illuminated
shades of yellow and green leaves
of trees rustling faintly in the distance
steep foothills and peaks
sweet fragrance of evening jasmine
a lone peacock calling out

sky--a lovely pale pink
fading like jewels
in evening light
the sun drops behind the hills
a gentle aroma drifts here
everything glows
like a kaleidoscope
of exquisite colors

## For all the sweet things

For all the sweet things
You have a memory,
A flower that bloomed
And can never fade,
Because of what it gave you
Pure Love and Joy

There is beauty in every corner of the world
Like the leaf in her hands she blows
It makes you stop
And think for a moment

Beauty and infiniteness
Of a single moment
Feeling the very essence
Nothing else matters

In the early morning light,
A beautiful flower awakens
To see the world in such a way,
Beauty from a single seed

Something wasn't the same anymore. Something had been opened up in me. Here I stood and everything before me seemed so alive than ever, the sun on me, the grass, flowers and trees around, the birds, the sky and earth. I was beginning to feel a connection I hadn't before. It is just like how a flower blossoms and lets the light touch it.

**Illusion**

All that you had ever known
All that you had ever believed
Was a forgotten dream
The world is more unreal
Than you thought it to be

No one outside of your Self
Only you, only you
The world consumes you
But you can break free
Break free

**You are**

You ask, you say,
You realize.
You are living light,
Luminosity of the moon.
Open the book, the window.
You are.

Tell yourself
The truth of who you are.

The key lies within.
You search and search.
Find yourself for yourself.

"Where can it be?" you ask.
It has always been here.
There is something beautiful
To one's eyes.
You are.

The most beautiful gem is
In the heart
And that is "life",
The essence of you.
You are.

You ask, you say, you realize.
You are living light,
Luminosity of the moon.
Open the book, the window.
You are.

## Wilderness

Follow the path.
You find yourself
All alone.
Darkness.
There is no one
Else around.

You look around.
You look above,
See Light peering through,

The branches of the trees
On you.
You are not alone.

You touch the dust,
Find this is where
It all starts
From a common ground.

**Finding**

You find yourself letting go.
You want to be free.
As a child, life carries with it magic.
Everything is so alive then,
But when a child is no longer a child,
That passion dies. The magic of life dies.
Everything becomes concrete.

The minutes go by
As do the hours and the days,
Months and years.
Before you know it,
You are older,
But when you look at yourself
You feel as if
It was just yesterday
You discovered what it means to live.

You look around
And examine life very closely.
It wasn't just the dialogues,
The sounds or the movements.
There was more.

You would see people smiling,
Laughing--all these emotions,
But it wasn't just the people.
You would feel yourself letting go.
You would see lovers
And feel the pain of their separation.
There was a whole world in you
And before you.

You had found love
And fell in love with love itself.
You would listen
And see everything before you.
You had found yourself.
The child always remains
With us and you then
See the truth for what it really is.

*Note: That child is the life of us, what we live to breathe for.*

**Our right to be**

Wherever I turn about,
The wind moves alongside me.
I look into myself and to nature.
What song am I to sing, but of our lives?
What is this story which you call "life"?
She questions and wonders
Dreaming of her tomorrow.

I feel the pain of a world
Lost in its own illusion
Of what is life.
The world makes it seem

There is a difference in you
And the rest
When all that is Real and free
Is the Self,
Behind all the covers,
An essence without labels.
There are no lines to draw.
See into the life of things.

We have our own universe,
Our own reality, what to be,
What the world wants us to be.
There are pages of a book
Of what seems to be real.
There are structures we've built,
To pull the threads out
Of this fabric of life
You are told to be different.

Looking back at the life in the mirror today
You find a reflection of something else.
Somewhere down the road
And you remember this wasn't it.
You let it go, but why?

There is an inner reflection
Of the truth behind all things
That the world outside
Cannot see.
The world stops listening,
But you can go on,
Because there is no difference.
We have our right to be.
So, don't hide or let it be hidden.
Unlock those doors.

There is something precious.
There is infinite beauty.
You can break through
Images of illusion.

Pain and fear are choices
Born of delusion.
You can create beauty
And learn to be
Part of all that is,
Because we have a right to be.

It was then
I looked in the mirror
And saw myself.
I touched the mirror
And felt fine glass.
How real is it?
Are you the one that you are?
Through the looking glass...I see
I am a story in myself.
We come out into this world
With stories of our lives.
What is this story called life?

There is an individual,
Who looks up to the infinite
Universe and into herself.
There is a dream in you
you just have to believe

Some think they know themselves,
But they don't accept themselves,
They crave to be what they are not.
We live in a world full of people

Trying to be who they are not.

There is a world that categorizes
Seeing you from the outside,
Not knowing who you are,
Not hearing you.
Where there is a heart,
Who is to listen?

We abide in a world
Where ethnocentrism is a cryptogram.
Cultures are unique
And contribute to the daily lives
Of what lives.

You have to remember
The sun will shine brightly
If you truly believe it.
Wherever you may go,
Wherever you may be,
You can succeed if you truly believe
And preserve that belief through faith.

We are all given a sense of individuality.
We have inherited this individuality.
We are ourselves.
And what does it take to be one's self?

One should remain true to one's self,
Not be another.
Why be another when one has himself?
It is great enough to have what one has been given,
To be blessed with life,
So that one may lead himself
Through the world to reach his aspirations.

You just have to believe.

And today you ask yourself
Which road to go.
You have it in you to choose.
The world will give what it can,
But it's for you to decide.

**I see the Truth**

I was told a story
I listened
And saw the Sun shine

I had a dream
Felt the Light on my eyes
Awoke
And saw the Sun rising

The sun, the sun, the sun
Shine
Melting in the distance
See the Truth

**Bliss**

This is the love of life,
Full of song,
Full of joy,
Full of harmony.

I hear the Voice of the Sea now.
It is the song of beauty,
The song of the flower

All under the sky.
It is a long journey home.
O, Voice of the Sea,
Hear my voice now,
Bliss.

The beauty of light,
The gem from up above,
Full of love and life,
Is hidden in the heart
Of all that is existence.
Call it bliss,
Sweetness divine
And eternity.

Sweet is thy voice
And thy smile upon that golden face.
Your fragrance wafts everywhere
Like rose dipped in honey and thy eyes shine
What is true, what is true.
Grace is upon every move.
Feel the gentle rhythm of the zephyrs
Through your hair,
Bliss.
See the beauty of all
Existence and Consciousness,
Bliss.

What is pure and untouched
The flower that never fades, Bliss.
Thy name is the nectar which I kiss,
Bliss.
This is the sea of thy love,
Bliss.

Carry me with it!
Bliss.

This is the message of the spirit,
Of essence and the life in me.
This is the light
Of this love, Bliss.

The winds blow everywhere
And carry with them a song.
There is a doorway.
Only you can find it.
It is of Being,
Of Love and Life,
Bliss.

Go through the passageway
And you will see the Light
That shows you the world,
Bliss.

There be a flower of love.
There be a wind to carry
The scent of the sea,
The Voice of the Sea.
There be a song of life, Bliss.

It is a long journey home.
Can you make it now?
O, Voice of the Sea,
Hear my voice now,
Bliss.

## The Rain

Something
Like the fragrance
Of incense
Here
At home

I stood looking
To the sky
For answers uncertain
Where to go

White clouds that
Transform to shades of grey
Dawn
And the sky

My eyes
The clouds
This ground
Green grass
And wildflowers

My hands
Shivering
This water
Rain
Dripping down

She turns around
Sings
Swirls in circles
With her scarf flying
All around her

Running through the fields
Free like the wind
Blowing her hair onto her face

If I must let go,
I must be free
Like the wind
Free
And this rain
That drips down

**A Long Road**

He knows the secret.
The rest is all an illusion.
The road to life is a long one.
You learn to experience,
Experience life.

We learn to be ourselves.
All experience teaches one
How to be what one is
And what one is meant to be.
All experience belongs to the Being
That one really is.

Be more than what life has been.
Freedom does not come on its own.
One must free oneself.
One must learn. It all starts here.

It's a long road.
When you know yourself, you know.
You know your path.
That path is what makes it happen.

It's a long road.
It is a long way home.
How we journey
Leaving our marks behind!

## Without the One

You see before you the beauty of it all. It is all there and within you, a stream of nectar in your heart. It is your breath of life. It is pure love and light. It is forever, Bliss and all that is. You are part of the art, a tapestry of life, that very greatness of life that makes your very existence possible. You are and will always be. Without the One, you are nothing. You are just a drop of the Sea, a drop of the Sea, but you make up that Wholeness of the Sea.

## River of Light

For long one searched for the meaning.
For long one denied the call that called him forth.
"If only summer could last longer," she said,
"Like the drawings in a sketchbook,
Whose imprints mark memories behind."

She remembered the slant of the summer sunset:
A red-ochre diffusion, against the cool blue of the sky,
Whose reflections could be seen in the still water
Of the ravine, the river of light.
Such settings have an allure that time cannot estimate.

She watched the events unfolding before her,
A drama in play with the illumination
Of the cloud-scuffed sky,
That was draped in a curtain of coppery gold

By the light of the melting sun.
"If only summer could last longer," she said, again.

She knew that even if the autumn hues were nearby,
She would remember and recall
The visions before her and the violet
Of the coming dusk.
And what if all that was perceived was an illusion?
Reality is beyond conception,
And so Truth is like the vastness of the valley.

An iris goes off to sleep as eve approaches
With breezes carrying the scent
Of flowers and luminous stars overhead.
How much longer would this stream run?
There is no ending to day,
But just an idea known as "yesterday".
Catch the ethereal colors of the day
And imprints they will be made.

She too was dust
As her form would be dust
Without the Light.
It was her soul that lived on
And carried a river of light
Like the soul of every other.

So many disguises,
And this was one of hers.
How many others she had
Before this were countless births
Long forgotten.
She was ever the same
Even with time changing.

The leaves would begin to fall
With the colors of autumn.
Once again tomorrow would rise.

Even then, the river of light would be shining.
Yesterday does not leave.
It is one of the many marks
That make today.

All that is in existence
Is the carrier of dust.
Dust, dust everywhere!
What lights up the many worlds
Is not the sun, but what is in all, the soul.
It is not about yesterday or tomorrow,
But today, the "now".

What beginning? What ending?
They speak of such, but who is to believe?
One is the maker of his own kismet.
And she asked, "What is this world leading to?"
Answers leaped at her. She could answer for herself.

Let go and go on.
Go downstream or upstream.
Pave your own path.
Summer will come again.
The river of light will still be here.
She must go on, and the memories
Would be with her.
Consciousness doesn't change.

Some gave it a name; others gave it no identity.
Some believed; others did not.

And then came a day when one looked
At his reflection in the river.
The perceptions perceived and lost
One knew there was a bigger picture.

The reflection looked back. "Who are you?" she asked.
It was the soul that shined more than anything else.
"I have found you!" she cried.
She had found the Truth for herself,
"I am that Consciousness."

## The sun shines on me

The sun shines on me
Shines on me
Dancing
In the sea of your love
Carry me on

Let it shine, let it shine
The light shines in your eyes
As the sun shines on me

The rays of the sun dance
In the endless sky of desire
You want to fly
You want to see
The sun shines on me

## Eyes

I stood there in the rain
Felt the rain on my hands
Looked at my hands
Show me the way

There's something more
Nothing here anymore
There's something more
Look into my eyes

Those eyes
I see those eyes

As I close my eyes
Those eyes

When she opened her eyes
She saw something more
I see those eyes
There's something more
When I can look up into those eyes
I know there's something more

In my life, you showered love,
Filled it with dreams
And the hope to be
And to become

In every sign of life, I found you
I saw something more
I got what I thought I had lost
Something more

I closed my eyes
Opened my eyes
And found a flower in my hands

**Beautiful**

Beautiful to the eyes
Beautiful to the mind
Beautiful you say
This heart

Beautiful it is
When you're outside
And the rain falls down
On you

Beautiful it is
When the sun shines
And you feel its warmth
On you

Beautiful are the colors
That mark the day
Beautiful are these words
If only you knew
Beautiful

## A few moments

I don't know why
But when I look inside
I feel
I see you

Just a few moments
A few moments to realize
That you had it all along
In you

Was it the fragrance
Of the flower you smelled?
Or the ray of light shining from the Sun?
You felt it in you
And knew it in a few moments of time

Was it the wind that blew all the leaves away?
Was it the rain that fell
Or the rainbow that I saw?
I don't know why
But when I look inside
I feel I see you

Just a few moments
A few moments to realize
That you had it all along
In you

**My heart sings a song**

My heart sings a song
Yearns for this Love,
you

In the moment,
For the moment,
My heart sings
For you

For you, for you, I am
For the stars in the night sky,
For the moonlight,
And early morning's light,
For the sun that shines,
My heart soars up high

For you, for you, I am
My heart sings a song,
Yearns for this Love, you
For you, for you, I am

**The sun is setting away**

The sun is setting away
As I look away to the sky
Always looking, always finding
The colors and a light breeze

A feeling of love in the heart
To hide it all away
And still to be
I cannot escape

A tear that finds its way
Like a pearl drop
From the sky
On my eyes
To kiss away the tears
To kiss away the pain
Take away, take away

Left alone
The world is not your guide
You are your own
You find the sun gone
But you know it's there
Waiting for tomorrow
It will be here
That touch and
The wind blows
There is more to life
But no
I believe in this

Eyes closed
I fall
Lying on the ground
Light of the moonshine
In this garden
I pray
What to cry out loud
And now another tear
Will you kiss it away

Just kiss it away

**For This**

Trying to be,
Trying to see
All our lives
For this, for this
I remain

The words on my lips remain
My heart desires for a bit of you
Why, oh why, this mind and this heart

Spring brings with it life
I want to be, to see
A bit of you
For this, for this
I remain

Is it for this desire
Trying to be,
Trying to see
All of our lives?

We all go our own ways
And sometimes we meet
Then we part

The dreams, the desires
The words on my lips remain
My heart desires for a bit of you
Why, oh why, this mind and this heart

## Sometimes you find yourself

Sometimes you find yourself
Walking alone
Sometimes you don't want to
Anymore
When everything that was
Was always it
Is no more
But you have to keep faith
And believe
Just as all things pass,
New things come
And everything will be alright

## Waiting

All our lives
We stand waiting for something
To come along our way
When that something is already there
All we need to do is try

## A gift awaits

A barren road with no one there,
Just the leaves of autumn
Lying on the ground
This feeling that leaves you
In this stillness, silence
Just a moment

And everything is taken away
But even when there seems to be
Nothing more
A gift awaits, the present

**Lesson of Life**

Life is a lesson. You learn every step of the way, sometimes holding hands, sometimes all alone, all alone!

You fall, you hurt. There are wounds, there are scars. Dreams are shattered and truths become lies. Promises that were said, but never kept.

What you hold onto, what you thought to be, was never what it used to be.

Every step of the way you stand, you live. It doesn't take much to lose it all; but, it takes much to gain.

Strength, strength, don't fall, don't drown. Life is with you, when everyone and everything might not be.

The past is behind you. Don't let it catch up with you. Run, you have the moment to live - to live!

You don't need the mirror to live. You don't need the reflection to tell you. You have it all in your heart.

Say, it's all up to you now to guide the way, to show the stars that couldn't be seen, because no one looked close enough. But you knew and saw it through.

Show the world there is truth, there is beauty, because life is with you.

It's when you are through, you learn it - Life!

*Note: Previously published in theEclectics, Vol. 10 (September 2006 issue) by Creative with Words Publications.*

## Faith

See the jasmine, you
Its sunshine, you
The blue sky, you
The sweet melody
Carried by the wind, you
Sweet honey, you

It takes faith to believe,
And it is with faith
That one believes
In anything at all

Feel it, the wonder in every object of the world
Every breath flowing, this heart beating
Every thought arising, speaking
Every flower and its fragrance
Every gentle breeze blowing
Everything
It takes faith
To believe
In anything at all

## Beliefs

There is so much to believe and not to believe within oneself and outside of oneself. We create our dreams out of our beliefs, because it is our beliefs that lead us to our desired pathways.

## *In Memory of a Star*

*(A tribute to Michael Jackson)*

Like a dream you came
Like a dream you left
Leaving your mark on the world
For the words you wrote
the songs you sang
the dream you danced
the love you poured out
Giving hope to the world
the life you lived
The song still carries out its tune
As the skies tell this story
in memory of a star

He danced the dream
Made us believe
that if you feel you can
if you really desire
it can be true
All you have to do is
start with you
showing us that we can
change the world
Showing us
that it wasn't just a song or dance
but becoming that song and dance
making it real to what we feel
that change starts right here
with you, with us
to "heal the world"

Come on now, don't you see
people making up stories
It doesn't matter what they say

That's all they do anyway
But you showed you were more
than talk
You showed us true
I don't care what people say
You made it beautiful
"dancing the dream"
with your songs and music
living it through

Beautiful was the dream
the words, the song
the steps, the dance
what you made it to be
Magical
that together it was one
As the words became a song
with the rhythm, music
with steps all melting
into a dance complete
left with a sense of peace
'Cause you made it right
As the dream became
coming together with the rest
As you said "We are the world"
and the words remain with us

Stars bloom at night
but you are a star that lit up even day
A dreamer whose dream came true
you came with a dream
left a dream with us
See the star dancing in the sky
twinkling with the light you are
back home to the river
As the skies tell this story
in memory of a star

## *Conclusion*

Life, beautiful, see and realize. This is the moment. Live in it, believe and make the most out of it. Like the flower that sends out its fragrance and never fades, like the song of sweetness, life itself sings such a beautiful song with the warmth of the sunshine, the gentle breeze that blows, the scent of freshly cut grass, the sound of rain, the ocean waves, the very earth that you feel with your hands. Every moment is infinite in itself. Life has much to offer. All you have to do is reach out.

Life is a living tapestry of motion like a film, but it has no start or finish. It gives you so much, embracing and filling your every moment and experience. You just have to see. It's up to you what you want to do with it. Life is a gift. Without it, where would you be? Whatever is, is a blessing and a gift. Remember, you have it in you to be. Life is to be and to become, to take action and make dreams become reality. Dream what you want to dream. Believe what you want to believe. Become what you want to become. The moment is now. You have yourself to be.

## *Some Artwork by Jasmine*

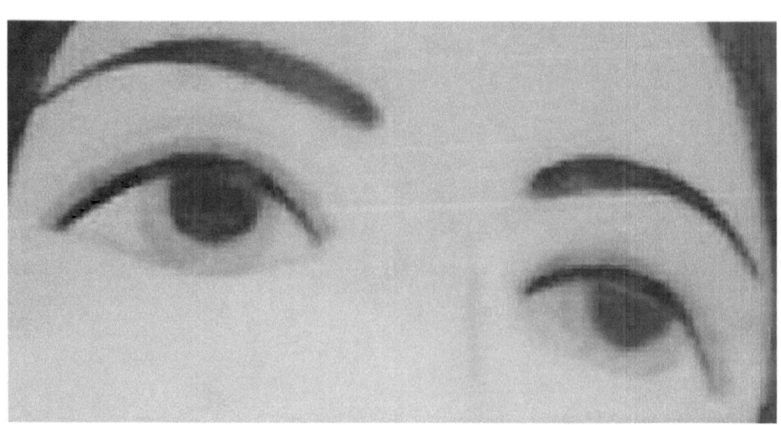

www.ingramcontent.com/pod-product-compliance
Ingram Content Group UK Ltd.
Pitfield, Milton Keynes, MK11 3LW, UK
UKHW041917190726
13854UKWH00003B/1284